The Parthenon at Nashville

THE PARTHENON OF PERICLES
And Its
REPRODUCTION IN AMERICA

For Mrs E. F. Lowry,
with best wishes,
B. F. Wilson III
Nov 28, 1947.

The Parthenon of Pericles
And Its
Reproduction in America

By
BENJAMIN FRANKLIN WILSON III
DIRECTOR OF THE PARTHENON

Illustrated

PARTHENON PRESS
NASHVILLE

THE PARTHENON OF PERICLES
And Its
REPRODUCTION IN AMERICA
Copyright, MCMXXXVII
By Benjamin Franklin Wilson III

Set Up, Electrotyped, Printed, and Bound
By the Parthenon Press at Nashville,
Tennessee, United States of America

C

To

MAJOR E. C. LEWIS

WHO CONCEIVED THE IDEA,

AND TO

THE MEMBERS OF THE BOARD OF PARK
COMMISSIONERS

1920-1937

R. M. DUDLEY	CHARLES M. McCABE
M. T. BRYAN	PERCY WARNER
LEE J. LOVENTHAL	ROGERS CALDWELL
W. R. COLE	J. P. W. BROWN
R. T. CREIGHTON	EDWIN WARNER
	C. A. CRAIG

WHOSE INTELLIGENT AND UNTIRING INTER-
EST MADE POSSIBLE THE REPRODUCTION
OF THE PARTHENON AT NASHVILLE; IN
MEMORY OF THOSE WHO ARE GONE,
AND IN APPRECIATION OF THOSE
WHO ARE LIVING, THIS VOLUME
IS GRATEFULLY DEDICATED

CONTENTS

THE PARTHENON OF PERICLES

x

PREFACE

FOR CENTURIES before and after its destruction, the Parthenon of Pericles has been of world-wide interest. Its reproduction at Nashville, Tennessee, has been of equal interest, especially as it is the only one in the world that represents the original as it stood on the Acropolis at Athens in the fifth century B.C.

The reproduction at Nashville is the result of years of intense investigation which revealed many inaccuracies, not as yet corrected, in the literature of the world.

In the six years since its opening to the public I have delivered to schools and colleges and cultural organizations formal lectures covering the history, architecture, and sculptures of the Parthenon. Many requests from members of these audiences from time to time have come to me, largely from educators, suggesting that I put the subject matter of the lectures into book form.   It is in response to these requests, and a desire to bring the Parthenon in its latest interpretation to the public, that I now present this volume.   I sincerely hope that it will bring pleasure to all who read it and prove of value to those teachers who wish to emphasize the history of an age that has never been excelled in the beauty of its architecture and sculptural art.

BENJAMIN FRANKLIN WILSON III.

The Parthenon,
Nashville, Tennessee, U. S. A

CHAPTER I

Background

THE PARTHENON OF PERICLES, while not thought to be one of the wonders of the world, nevertheless has always been regarded as one of the most wondrously beautiful and inspiring of the world's buildings. It embraces the best effort of the mind, the heart, and the hand of man. In it are bound up the religion, the history, and the art of Greece.

It has been well said that art is organized emotion, while science is organized knowledge. The field of emotion found its first great development among the Greeks, and in the time of Pericles reached its zenith. Assuredly the Greeks have never been ex-

celled in the beauty of their architecture or
sculptural art. In the field of science, however, we find another story, for in the building of the Parthenon the Greeks were
greatly handicapped by a lack of the knowledge of mechanics. The handling of the
great blocks of marble from the quarry far
below to the top of the Acropolis and the
putting in place of the great doors were for
them stupendous undertakings. Certainly
in this, our own goodly period of the prog-
ress of the world, we should not begrudge
the Greeks any glory that is justly theirs nor
discount their accomplishment by calling
attention to the fact that the Age of Pericles
was the "Golden Age of Greece." When
we contrast the many advantages possessed
by our own age, more wonderful does that
stand out. Lacking the benefits of modern
knowledge and invention in all branches of

the physical world, they produced results that challenge the best that we can do. Indeed, the labor, the patience, the skill, to say nothing of the inspiration that was theirs, force us to stand in amazement before the Parthenon of Pericles.

The influence of religion was dominant in the life and thought that produced such outstanding men in this period of the world's history as Phidias and Sophocles, Ictinos and Pericles. Every function of the mind, every activity of the hand, was closely associated with some god or goddess, and to this inspirational incentive the world is largely indebted for the Parthenon.

The mythological stories of the Parthenon largely cover the mythology of Greece. Twenty-eight of the major deities and numerous minor deities and personifications adorn its pediments. The three Fates, a

13

group of east pediment figures, thought to be one of the most beautiful examples of sculptural art in the world, is a fine example of the influence of religion on Greek art. This wonderful group as it exists, eighty per cent perfect, in the British Museum today, is generally attributed to Phidias. The back of the group, although it was not to be seen, was made just as lovely as the front. The draperies of the figures and of the couch on which they repose, the figures themselves, all are as beautiful as the parts exposed to view. No doubt Phidias felt that his goddess knew that they were beautiful in their entirety and that was reward enough for him.

The Greeks in Pericles' day did not allow the imagination to run away with them. Every detail of the Parthenon, every line, bears silent witness to their moderation. They abhorred eccentricity. One of their proverbs, "No excess," is exemplified by the perfect harmony of the proportions of the Parthenon. They were great originators, but they did not hesitate to appropriate the wisdom and the art of preceding ages and of other peoples, and work them into their own conceptions. As a result of all this, they gave the world the Parthenon, which, no doubt, Plutarch had in mind when he wrote, some five hundred years later, "Every work of the time of Pericles had, from the moment of its creation, the beauty of an old master, yet retaining its freshness and newness to this day." He said: "There is a certain novelty that seems to bloom upon them, which ever keeps their beauty untouched by time, as if they had perpetual breath of life and an unaging soul, mingled in their composition."

At the time of its destruction, in the sev-

15

enteenth century, a little more than two thousand years after its completion, the Parthenon was in almost as good condition as at its beginning. The changes made by the Christians in the fifth century and by the Turks in the fifteenth century had impaired it but little, all of which is eloquent testimony to the thoroughness with which the task was accomplished. The co-ordination of mind, hand, and heart of the Greeks of that age has never been excelled by men of any time and found its culmination in the Parthenon.

There are two schools of thought with regard to the creation of the Parthenon. One, which is predominantly mathematical, holds to the theory that it was the result of the super-mathematical ability of the Greeks of that day. It maintains that all the proportions of the building, resulting in har-

16

The Parthenon at Nashville at Night

mony nowhere else equaled, were the direct result of calculation, and that all its architecture was made to conform to certain mathematical formulas. The other group holds to the opinion that the Parthenon is the result of the experience of the ages, the aestheticism of the age in which it was built and the genius of Phidias who built it, all resulting in the subtleties and refinements that make it the most perfect building in the world from an architectural standpoint, conforming to, but not a result of, certain mathematical formulas. To this latter school adhere those responsible for the reproduction of the Parthenon at Nashville, and those also who live in the atmosphere created by it.

In the year of our Lord eighteen hundred and ninety-six nothing remained of the Parthenon at Athens save an old ruin, rapidly decaying. Slumbering in Greece and in the hearts of cultured men and women throughout the world, there remained a lingering regret for the glory that had once been hers. Far off to the west, in a land undreamed of in Phidias' day, and in a city likewise cultured, Nashville, Tennessee, "The Athens of the South," there stirred in the heart of a man this memory of a bygone glory and there was born a happy thought that resulted, in 1931, in a new creation of the Parthenon in the Western World. This time the creation was not on an acropolis, that echoed to the rhythmic marching of the Pan-Athenaic Procession, but in a beautiful landscape of blooming flowers, green grasses, and waving trees, its lovely east pediment mirrored in the placid waters of Lake Watauga, its corridors echoing to the happy voices of children at play or of lovely

18

young women as they render some pageant commemorating the days of Ancient Greece.

The Parthenon at Nashville, this Queen of the Western World, this Alpha and Omega of perfect architecture, was the result of many years of research and study on the part of inspired architects, artists, and archaeologists. It was opened to the public on May 20, 1931. Since that time hundreds of thousands of visitors from every niche and corner of the world have trod its classic corridors and proclaimed its beauty.

There are several buildings in the world that resemble the Parthenon, notably the Lincoln Memorial at Washington and the Church of the Madeleine in Paris, yet only the Parthenon at Nashville is a perfect mirror of the original, as it stood in all its pristine beauty and glory on the Acropolis in

the closing days of the fifth century B.C.
and which must have inspired in the Greeks
of Pericles' day the mighty deeds in literature and art that characterized their history
in that age.

CHAPTER II

The Parthenon at Athens

THE PARTHENON was built on the Acropolis, a hill two hundred feet above the streets of Athens, in the year 438 B.C. Not yet had the blight of decay laid its hand upon an outstanding civilization, and Athens was at the zenith of her glory and power. The nations she had conquered contributed to her wealth and her slaves furnished the labor for her every great undertaking. It is no wonder that at this time she should turn her heart toward her beloved Athena and honor her with a shrine. Athena Parthenos was her name, hence the word Parthenon. She was the wisest and most beautiful of the Grecian deities and the Parthenon was her temple.

Coming down through the mists of the centuries, the handiwork of man constantly improved, as a natural consequence, with his intelligence. It is thought that the earliest Greeks worshiped their goddess without any temples, but with crude altars of uncut stone and unhewn wood. Gradually, as they became more intelligent, they began building temples, each one lovelier than the one before and all on the same foundation, as attested by excavations at Athens. It is not known just how many there were of this previous series of temples, covering as they did several thousands of years, but it is known that the last one was destroyed by the Persian Xerxes in the year 480 B.C. Then came the Parthenon, begun in 447 and dedicated to the goddess in 438. We know that some work was done on the Parthenon as late as 432 B.C., but the Peloponnesian War and a great plague that overspread Greece about that time interrupted any records that may have been made, if indeed any were made. At any rate the work on the Parthenon was far enough advanced in 438 to permit its dedication.

The Parthenon was built under the supervision of Phidias, the greatest artist of form the world has ever known. He was a close friend of Pericles, archon of Athens, who, appreciating Phidias' great executive ability, as well as his genius, commissioned him to build the temple. He had built a number of other temples for Pericles, notably the temple of Zeus at Olympia; but the Parthenon was the most ambitious of all his undertakings, as indeed it was the most ambitious of all the Greek temples. Phidias,

23

himself a sculptor, was ably assisted by Ictinos, an architect, and Kallicrates, a builder. Between the three they produced the old Parthenon, which up to that time had never been equaled in beauty and certainly has never been surpassed since. Here, for approximately a thousand years, the Greeks worshiped their goddess, and it was during this period that Greece produced the greatest of her philosophers, warriors, artists, and writers.

The Greeks were somewhat slow in embracing Christianity, but by 426 A.D. they had become a Christian nation. In the meantime Greece had fallen under the dominion of the Roman Empire and the Emperor Theodosius II changed the Parthenon into a Christian church. It is not known just what changes were made in the Parthenon at that time, but we know that

The Ruins of the Parthenon at Athens in 1929

the exterior was not altered and only minor changes were made in the interior.

From the experience of speakers in the Parthenon at Nashville it is certain that whatever changes were made came as a result of an effort to improve its acoustics. Tests prove that it is four times as difficult to speak in the Parthenon as in the average present-day auditorium. The Greek worship was semi-silent and acoustic excellence was not necessary. When the Christians began their worship, conditions were immediately changed and something must have been done about it.

For a little more than a thousand years the Greeks worshiped Jehovah in the Parthenon, when in the fifteenth century (1458 to be exact) there came the conquest by the Turks and the Parthenon was changed by them into a Mohammedan mosque. This time the interior was left much as it was and the changes confined to the exterior where minarets were added, after which the Turks worshiped their god Allah in the Parthenon for two hundred years.

It is thus seen that the Parthenon was always the temple of some god, the Pagan, the Christian, or the Mohammedan. The quiet restfulness induced by its classic architecture makes us wonder sometimes why more of the churches of the world have not imitated it instead of the almost universal use throughout the Christian Era of the loud arches of the Gothic.

In 1687 the Parthenon, except for the minor changes to the interior in the fifth century by the Christians and those of the exterior in the fifteenth century by the Turks, was almost in as good condition as

26

in the beginning. In that year the Turks were driven out of Athens by the Venetians, representing a Christian nation. In this war the Turks stored gunpowder temporarily in the Parthenon for safe keeping, thinking the gods of the Greeks, which adorned its pediments, would give them good luck. They had no particular reverence for the Greek gods, but rather attributed talismanic powers to them. However, a Venetian shot, not so respectful of the gods of the Greeks, struck the Parthenon and rendered it the interesting ruin that, for the most part, remains in Athens today.

Historians, especially those writing in our present-day encyclopaedias, and histories are more severe in dealing with the Turks than, it would seem from the facts, they deserve. As a result, the opinion is general that the Turks destroyed the Parthenon.

Taking into consideration the fact that for two centuries prior to the Venetian attack the Turks had worshiped their own god in the Parthenon, it seems certain they had no lack of reverence for the building. It is reasonable to assume that in their dire extremity, as a temporary measure only, they used the Parthenon as a storage place for their ammunition. There does not seem to be any good reason for fastening this stigma on the Turks who stored the gunpowder in it, rather than upon the Venetians who fired the shot which exploded the gunpowder and destroyed it. It would be nearer the truth to say that its destruction is chargeable to war.

As a result of the explosion, the entire interior was destroyed. The columns, the architrave, the ceiling, the roof, nothing remained except the floor and fragments of the walls. Fortunately the explosive agent was gunpowder, whose power acts upward and outward only; consequently the floor was not materially injured and the markings on the floor disclose the order of architecture, location, and diameter of the columns. If the explosive agent had been our modern dynamite, it would have destroyed the interior and made it difficult to reproduce, particularly as all the columns of the building differ in size and spacing.

The exterior did not suffer as much from the force of the explosion as did the interior. Of the fifty-eight columns on the outside, forty-four were left standing. Eight on the northeast corner and six on the south side were entirely blown away. A few of the end columns were damaged slightly.

Almost all of the pedimental sculptures were blown off, injuring them greatly. It

29

is said that the horses of the west pediment, magnificent examples of art, survived the explosion; but General Morosini, the Venetian commander, in an effort to salvage them let them fall from the building to an almost total loss. Only two fragmentary groups of the pedimental sculptures are left on the old ruin. Plaster casts of these are in the British Museum.

In 1929 the Greek government, with the assistance of American capital, began a restoration of the Parthenon. It seems unfortunate that this particular time should have seen the beginning of so worth-while an effort, since it also marked the advent of a world-wide financial depression. Owing to this handicap, the work of restoration has been slow. The work done up to 1937 has resulted in the replacement of the columns blown from the northeast corner of the

Parthenon and the repair of the damage to those on the ends. Nothing has been done to the interior, and the building is still open to the skies. It is to be hoped that the Greeks will not allow anything to prevent the completion of the work. The people of the entire world, especially those of America, look on with good wishes for the restoration in the Old World of that which has already been given to the New.

CHAPTER III

The Parthenon at Nashville

∽∾

IN THIS AGE of eager restlessness, constant experiment, and changing fashions, it is essential that we should have some standards of the beautiful preserved to us that are beyond question or criticism. Such a standard existed in the Parthenon at Athens, and the people of America and of the world are indeed fortunate in its reproduction at Nashville, where it stands as a beacon light to men and women of every land who are interested in the culture of the past, the present, or the future.

In 1896 the State of Tennessee had attained its full century of statehood. To celebrate that important event in the life of the State, an exposition was held in Nashville known as the Tennessee Centennial Exposition. As is often the case, the preparation of the Exposition was delayed for a year and not until 1897 were the gates thrown open to visitors. The Director General[1] of the Exposition Company conceived the idea of having as the Gallery of Fine Arts for the Exposition a reproduction of the Parthenon at Athens. This was indeed a happy thought, as it culminated eventually in marking a period in the history of the art of the world. Nashville, on account of its many schools and colleges and accompanying culture, had long been known as the "Athens of the South." It is not

[1] Major E. C. Lewis, a highly cultured and successful business executive of Nashville, himself an architect and lover of art.

surprising then that such a thought should have found lodgment in the heart of a man noted for his culture and love of art.

In the successful prosecution of the work of reproduction there was no time for research and study. Relying on existing information and records, and upon the ruin at Athens, a very creditable building was erected of laths and plaster, in the few months available. No attempt was made to reproduce the interior or the sculptures of the Parthenon. The exterior, however, was not so difficult, as it was largely revealed by the ruin at Athens and was much the same as that of the present Parthenon at Nashville. The building was whitewashed and was a most beautiful sight to those visiting the Exposition.

The "Gallery of Fine Arts" attracted so much favorable attention during the

Exposition that at its close the people of Nashville, who had become greatly attached to it, insisted that it should not be torn down when the other buildings were destroyed. Later the Board of Park Commissioners obtained possession of approximately one hundred and fifty acres of land surrounding the old building and laid out what is now beautiful Centennial Park.

Built to last a year, the much-loved Gallery of Fine Arts stood for nearly twenty-four years, used at times for art exhibits until, in spite of every effort made for its preservation, it became a greater ruin than its prototype in Athens. The Park Board had long had as a cherished objective the reproduction of the Parthenon in permanent materials. This was an ambitious undertaking even for a city much larger than Nashville, and it was not until 1920 that the old building was torn down and on its site the present reproduction of the Parthenon at Athens begun.   Competent architects,[2] artists,[3] and archaeologists[4] were employed who devoted the best efforts of their careers to the work.   No effort was too great, no money was spared to make the Parthenon as near as humanly possible

[2] Mr. Russell Hart, of the firm of Hart, Freeland and Roberts, gave eleven years of his life to this great work.

[3] Belle Kinney, a Nashville woman, and her husband Leopold Scholz, an Austrian sculptor, attained national fame by the work done on the pediments of the Parthenon.   The metopes were the work of George J. Zolnay of Washington, D. C.

[4] Mr. Dinsmoor of New York represented the architects in the archaeological work on the Parthenon and contributed much to the world's knowledge of it.   Some of his discoveries resulted in reversing previously accepted ideas of the Parthenon.

a reproduction of the original as it existed when it was the temple of Athena in the fifth century B.C. The result has been the creation at Nashville of a marvelous world shrine.

The chief difference between the original and the reproduction lies in the character of the materials of which they were made. The Parthenon at Athens was built of Pentelic marble quarried nearby, while that at Nashville is of reinforced concrete finished by a patented process which, under the influence of electric lights, very closely resembles marble. The Pentelic marble of the original had a small content of iron which, in the passage of time, became oxidized and the color of the ruin at Athens is now a brownish yellow from the iron oxide stain.

By the use of reinforced concrete in the building at Nashville three important ad-

vantages were obtained: durability, econo-
my, and the privilege of seeing the Parthenon in two colors. Reinforced concrete is
the most durable of all building materials
and at the same time the most economical.
By a careful selection of materials, the color
of the Parthenon at Nashville in daylight is
brownish yellow, the same as the ruin at
Athens. This effect was obtained by using,
as the aggregate of the concrete, a brownish
yellow gravel from the bottom of the Poto-
mac River in Virginia. The Parthenon is
floodlighted for an hour and a half each
night and is said to be the best floodlighted
building in America. Under the influence
of the floodlights the concrete is rendered
the color of marble and the visitor sees the
Parthenon at Nashville as Pericles saw it at
Athens. The Parthenon at night is indeed
a beautiful sight, one of the most beautiful

in the world. A writer in one of the leading newspapers of America, in describing the Parthenon as he saw it illuminated, had this to say: "If I am ever so fortunate as to reach the Pearly Gates of the New Jerusalem, I shall expect to find nothing more radiantly beautiful than the Parthenon at Nashville at night." In getting this highly realistic effect the engineers have, with indirect lighting, slightly darkened the outer walls of the building by concealing a fringe of red lights, of relatively small intensity, in the ceiling of the corridors and porticos. This gives to the walls a rosy hue, furnishing a darker background for the better casting of the shadows of the columns upon it by the intense white floodlights and at the same time accentuating the whiteness of the remainder of the building.

The Parthenon at Nashville is as near as

possible a reproduction of the Parthenon of Pericles; yet, in addition to the difference in the materials of which they were built, several modern innovations have been introduced, designed to add to the convenience and comfort of the visitors, but which in no wise detract from its beauty of form. Among these is a modern system of heating and ventilation, concealed in the thick walls of the building. The heating plant at Nashville is twelve hundred feet away from the Parthenon itself. Other differences will be noted in succeeding chapters as they occur in the narrative.

The chief regret at Nashville has been that there was no acropolis on which to locate the Parthenon. This defect in the setting has been to some extent atoned for by building it adjacent to a small lake and surrounding it with a beautiful park. The

41

Parthenon is a sacred thing in the eyes of the people of Nashville, and the park, needless to say, is kept at the highest point of beauty possible.

The Parthenon at Athens had no basement; but in the reproduction at Nashville a basement has been added to house a museum of fine arts so as not to violate the spirit of the Parthenon, which was always a temple of some god, by placing paintings upon its walls. Unfortunately, for lack of funds, only two rooms of the basement have been completed at present, comprising one-seventh of the available space. One of these rooms is used as a lecture room and the other houses the James M. Cowan [5] Collection of

[5] The Cowan Collection was presented to his native State, to be housed in the Parthenon forever, by Mr. James M. Cowan of Aurora, Illinois. He was born and reared in Tennessee, but spent

Art. This collection consists of sixty-three original oil paintings by American artists, [6] very carefully selected to make it a cross section of American art, every period of which is represented by one or more outstanding artists.

The approach to the basement is by two stairways each leading from the east ends of the interior corridors. Visitors going down these stairways are as effectually out of the Parthenon as though they went down the steps on the outside of the building. When the basement is completed the Par-

the most of his life in Illinois, where he was a successful man of business and a patron of art.

[6] The Collection was selected for the donor by Mr. Walter Leighton Clark of the Grand Central Art Galleries of New York, who was one of America's outstanding connoisseurs and art patrons and who was largely responsible for Mr. Cowan's generous act.

thenon will become the art center of the South.

Begun in 1920, the research necessary to make the Parthenon a reproduction of the original as it was in the beginning, required eleven years for completion. In 1925 the exterior was finished and, as has already been said, the Parthenon was thrown open to the public on May 20, 1931, six years having been necessary to complete the interior.

As the representative in the New World of the finest classic art of the Old, the Parthenon is not alone an asset of Nashville but of the whole of America.

CHAPTER IV

Description of the Parthenon

IN THE FOLLOWING CHAPTERS covering the general description of the Parthenon, its architecture and its sculptures, the descriptions are of the building at Nashville which correspond closely to those of the original, the exceptions being noted in every instance.

The Parthenon of Pericles has been shown in a new light as a result of the eleven years of research and study put into the Parthenon at Nashville. Some of the older conceptions were conclusions rather than the result of research. For the first time the modern Greek who visits Nashville sees the

Parthenon as his ancestors saw and admired it at Athens.

The average person on his first visit to the Parthenon is certain to have his emotions stirred by the sight of it. He is impressed with the beauty of the ensemble, the harmony of its proportions, and with a sense of its stability and strength. His wonder grows with the closeness of his contact.

The Parthenon is sixty-five feet high with its superstructure resting on the base or stylobate of the temple, consisting of three steps. The largest dimensions are furnished by the lowest of these steps, which is two hundred and thirty-eight feet long by one hundred and eleven feet wide. The top step, on which rests the peristyle, is two hundred and twenty-eight feet long by one hundred and one feet wide.

One of the most interesting peculiarities,

or, it might be said subtleties, employed by the Greeks in building the Parthenon, is that no two major lines are exactly parallel nor are they exactly equal in length. As an example of this, the exact length of the east top step of the Parthenon is 101.341 feet, while that of the west top step is 101.-363 feet. This 101.341 feet is the equivalent of the Greek hundred feet and is thought to be the ancient Greek standard of length.

Another interesting thing about the east top step of the Parthenon is that its length is exactly that of a second of latitude at the Equator. Before we give the Greeks too much credit for their knowledge of geography and mathematics however, we should reflect that in Pericles' day they thought the earth was flat and therefore knew nothing of latitude and longitude; it was merely a strange coincidence.

The most striking feature of the Parthenon when viewed from any exterior approach is the encircling row of great Doric columns forming the peristyle. There are forty-six of these columns, seventeen on each side, six on each end, not counting the corner columns twice, and six each on the east and west porticos. The columns of the peristyle are thirty-four feet high with an approximate diameter at the base of six feet. They have an average spacing from face to face of eight feet. The columns of the porticos are somewhat smaller, with a base diameter of five and one-half feet.

The main body of the building is called the cella. The exterior walls of the cella, on the long sides, form with the columns majestic corridors. The shadows falling on the

Shadows on the Parthenon at Nashville showing the "Greek Urn" in End of
Exterior Corridor

Showing a Section of East Portico with Closed Doors

walls and floors of the corridors at certain times of the day are very beautiful. It is said that the old Greeks told the time of day by the shadows of the Parthenon, which was easily visible from any part of Athens.

Another interesting feature connected with the corridors is what has come to be known as the "Greek Urn." This is the figure cut in the sky by the columns and architrave at the ends of the long exterior corridors. This figure is found between every two Doric columns inside and out, but is most perfectly seen at the ends of the corridors on the long side where distance lends perspective. The Greek Urn has been made famous in literature by the poet Keats in his "Ode to a Grecian Urn." It is said that he was inspired to write this poem by an inspection of the Elgin marbles in the British Museum.

The only openings to the Parthenon are the two pairs of great bronze doors leading off the east and west porticos. These doors are the largest in America and probably the largest bronze doors in the world. They can only be challenged, as to size, by the Congressional Library doors at Washington or by those of one of the old Cathedrals in Florence, Italy; and they are slightly larger than either. The doors are twenty-four feet high, seven feet each wide, a foot thick, and weigh seven and one-half tons each. They are exactly like the old Greek doors, with three exceptions, which are all modern innovations. The first of these is found in the way in which they are hung on posts running through the hinges, on either side, with three sets of ball bearings in each hinge, making them so easily opened that a four-year-old child can push them open. The original doors were opened on rollers under the bottom of the doors running on semi-circular brass tracks set in the floors of the east and west rooms. Needless to say they were opened with difficulty and probably required the combined strength of all the Greeks that could get around them to handle them. A Yale lock on the outside, which of course is modern, harmonizing with the ball bearings, and the ability to split one of the doors so as not to be compelled to open the entire door unless desired, form the only differences between the doors in the Parthenon at Nashville and those of the old Greek temple at Athens. Both sides of the doors are divided into three panels. On the outside, the lower panel is decorated with the head of a lion, the center panel has the head of the Medusa, and the top is decorated with a ram's head. On the inside, each of the panels contains a simple Greek design.

There is no doubt that the front entrance to the Parthenon was through the eastern doors. If there were no documentary evidence to prove this (and there is an abundance), the fact that all the twenty-two gods of the east pediment are major deities of the Greeks, while only four of those on the west pediment are major, the remainder being personifications and minor deities, would be sufficient proof that the eastern end was the front of the building.

Entering the Parthenon through the eastern doors, the visitor would most likely first note the division of the main body of the building, or cella, by a transverse wall dividing it into two rooms—the east room and the west room.

The east room is known as the Naos or

temple proper. It is ninety-eight feet long, sixty-three feet wide, with a ceiling height of forty-three feet. The most striking feature of the Naos is the double row of Doric columns, twenty-three below and twenty-three above, with an architrave between. These form a colonnade surrounding the main floor on three sides. The lower units of the colonnade are three and three-quarter feet in diameter at the base and twenty-one feet high. Those of the upper tier are two and a quarter feet in diameter and sixteen feet high. The columns on the long side of the colonnade form with the interior cella walls beautiful and impressive corridors.

In the original Parthenon the transverse wall was solid, with no communication between the east and west rooms; but in the Nashville reproduction there are two doors opposite the ends of the interior corridors to facilitate movement through the building and the display of its interior to the immense throngs that on special days visit the Parthenon. It is easy to imagine the difficulty which would be entailed without them since on many occasions there have been from three to five thousand visitors in a single day.

Another interesting feature is that the floor of the corridors is raised an inch and a half above the main floor of the Naos. We must look beyond the days of Pericles for an explanation of this particular construction. In Pericles' day the Greeks built their homes and public buildings with roofs and the Parthenon itself had a thin marble slab roof. At an earlier time, however, they built the most of their homes and all their public buildings around an open court, or patio, and when it rained the Greeks moved back under the corridors in security while the depressed floor carried off the water. Phidias retained this inheritance from an earlier day, in the Parthenon of Pericles, simply as a contribution to its beauty.

In the west end of the Naos, twenty feet from the end columns, facing the eastern doors, stood the Chryselephantine Statue of Athena, the beautiful shrine of the temple, if historians of that day are to be believed. It was forty feet high and reached within three feet of the ceiling. It was made, as its name indicates, of gold and ivory. The fleshy parts were of carved ivory and the remainder were plates of gold suspended on a framework of cedarwood. It was the masterpiece of Phidias and was worth a king's ransom.

When Theodosius II changed the Parthenon into a Christian church in the fifth century he moved the statue of Athena to Byzantium, capital of the Roman Empire, as of course it would have been incongruous to leave it in the Parthenon after the change in religions. No doubt it was quite welcome in Byzantium. After the removal of the Chryselephantine Statue its fate is shrouded in mystery. It is thought that it was destroyed either by vandals for the gold and ivory of which it was made or fell a victim to the great fire that devastated Constantinople in the latter part of the tenth century; at any rate, it has never been seen since. No part of it and no authentic sketch, drawing, or model of it has ever been found. We are dependent alone upon historical descriptions of the statue for our conceptions of it. The best known of these conceptions is perhaps that of the Romans, uncovered at Athens in

Top of Treasury or West Room Showing Ionic Columns and Decorations

Interior of Naos or East Room of Parthenon at Nashville Showing the Ceiling and Plaster Casts of Elgin Marbles

1880 and thought by some to be a copy of the original. Other conceptions are extant. For the reason that any reproduction of the Chryselephantine Statue would necessarily be speculative, those responsible for decisions as regards the Parthenon at Nashville have not been enthusiastic as to its reproduction.

The Greeks entered the eastern doors at the hour of temple worship, which was always in the early morning, bearing their gifts of gold and silver and other valuable articles. There they were met by the priests, who received the gifts. While the worshipers paid their devotions to the goddess at her shrine, the priests took their gifts through the great doors, thence along the exterior corridors, through the western doors, and into the west room where they deposited them. This room is called the Maiden's Chamber or Treasury. Athena was a virgin goddess, hence the term maiden. No one was permitted in this room except the priests and the authorities of the temple. It was in no sense a Holy of Holies as in the temple at Jerusalem, but was a place where the valuables were kept and consequently the masses of the people were excluded.

The west room is forty-four feet long and sixty-three feet wide. As in the east room, its most striking feature is contributed by the columns. There are four of these arranged in a rectangle sixteen by twenty-three feet in the center of the room. The columns are Ionic in design and, unlike those of the east room, are monoliths. They are forty-one feet high, six feet in diameter at the base and three and a half feet at the top. The decorations of the room are Ionic also, in contrast with those of the east room.

The decorations of the Parthenon are all

authenticated. Fragments of them are preserved in the British Museum, in the Louvre,
and some of the colors still show, though
dimly, on the protected parts of the ruin
at Athens. The decorations at the top of
both the interior and exterior architrave,
above and between the capitals of the Doric
columns, are technically known as guttae.
These are thought to be contemporary in
origin with the Doric columns and an evolution of the pegs with which the Egyptians
put their temples together in pre-pyramid
days.

The color decorations are principally in
shades of blue and red with some yellows.
In the interior the colors are found in the
fret along the top of the architrave in the
east room and in the moldings around the
ceilings of both rooms. The colors of the
exterior occur in the frets around the top

of the cella walls, in the ceiling of the corridors and porticos, and in the decorations of the cornice. Blue is the predominant color, and no wonder, for was not the blue-eyed Pallas Athena the patron goddess of Athens! The Greeks loved the blue of the skies which encircled Mount Olympus, where dwelt the most of their gods, and the reflected blue of the beautiful Aegean Sea where lived the remainder. Only in the background of the sculptures does the red predominate.

We are usually prone to think of the Greeks of this period as pre-eminently artists of form as attested by their beautiful statues and have but little regard for their use of color. An inspection of the colors of the Parthenon, however, forces us to the conclusion that they had quite an appreciation of color as well as of form.

The Greeks lighted the old temple almost wholly through the great doors which, as we have seen, are in each end of the building. Some of the older authorities suggested that there was no roof on the Parthenon and others thought there were openings in the cella walls at the junction point of the walls and ceilings for the admission of light and for ventilation. The weight of authority, however, is against any openings in the Parthenon other than the two great pairs of doors.

The building was so orientated that at the hour of temple worship, which was always in the early morning, the strong oriental sunlight could stream between the columns of the east portico and through the doors, thrown wide open, flooding the statue of Athena, where the plates of gold would catch the morning sunbeams and reflect them. This, with the help of small torches on tripods between the columns, furnished sufficient light for the temple worship, certainly as much as is found in the Gothic cathedrals of the present day with their stained glass windows.

At Nashville the lighting is entirely different, all coming from above, and this is one of the most prominent of the modern innovations incorporated in the Parthenon. The Greek ceiling was exactly like that at Nashville with this one exception: that while in the Greek temple the spaces between the great cedar beams that span the ceiling and support the roof was an open grillwork of cedarwood, at Nashville the open spaces have been filled with frosted panes of glass, etched to resemble the rays of the sun. The Greeks might have had glass, as the manufacture of plate glass by the Phoenicians antedated the period of Pericles by some five hundred years. As we have seen, however, they had no incentive to use it, for they obtained their light from below. The incentive at Nashville is to conceal the two hundred and seventy-two high-powered electric lights that give to the interior its beautiful simulation of sunlight, accentuating its beauty and, to a great extent, eliminating the shadows. The interior appears the same at midday as at midnight. Visitors in daylight hours are seldom able to detect that the ceiling is not a skylight, forgetting in their enthusiasm that there is a concrete roof on the building.

As has been said, the original Parthenon was covered with a thin marble slab roof. It has been suggested that some light for the interior came through the roof, citing the alabaster roofs of Egypt as an example.

63

However, it takes a rather vivid imagination to cause us to think that any appreciable amount of light could get through a marble slab, however thin it might have been. The roof at Nashville is like the one at Athens, except as to the material used in its construction. The antefixes along the eaves served the purpose of covering the joints between the marble slabs and are of carved ornamental design. At each corner of the roof is a lion's head, thought to be intended originally as a waterspout. Also at each corner of the roof is a stone block upon which is surmounted a Gryphon monster, standing guard over the temple day and night. The highest points on the Parthenon are the carved ornaments known as the Acroteria, at each end of the building above the pediments.

It is difficult for anyone to describe the

Parthenon and do it justice. Suffice it to say that it is "a thing of beauty and a joy forever." It has been the Alpha and Omega of architects in all succeeding generations and its classic lines are being copied in buildings throughout the world of today.

CHAPTER V

The Architecture of the Parthenon

◦◦◦

THE ARCHITECTURE OF GREECE was essentially Doric. The Ionic was an exotic in Athens and the Corinthian was more Roman than Grecian and found no place in the Parthenon. There is a total of one hundred and eight columns in the building, and of these all on the exterior and all in the east room, one hundred and four in number, are Doric, while the four in the west room are Ionic.

Standing in one of the doors between the east and west rooms, the visitor to the Parthenon can enjoy the beauty of the interior as well as compare the Doric and Ionic columns, noting their contrasts. The former rises directly from the floor without a base while the latter has an elaborate one. Both have fluted shafts which have the protection of entasis. Featuring the Doric column is a plain capital, while that of the Ionic is highly decorative. In spite of its simplicity, however, the Doric column has always been awarded the palm of beauty by both artists and architects, illustrating the truism that beauty unadorned is beauty superlative.

The story of the Parthenon would not be complete without giving, in part, the genesis of the Doric columns: Greece obtained the most of her architecture and all her columns from Egypt. When we think of Grecian civilization we think in terms of hundreds of years, for twenty-four hundred years have elapsed since the Parthenon was built. When we think of Egyptian civilization we think in terms of thousands of years, the Pyramids being five thousand or more years of age.

Man worked in wood long before he worked in stone, and when, in those old days, the Egyptians wished to build a temple they felled the great trees of the forest and brought their trunks with the bark still on them and placed them in the building for columns. In the evolution of time, these tree trunks have come down to us as the Doric columns of the Greeks. The prominent lines of the shafts of the columns, known technically as arris lines, represent the evolution of the bark of the tree, while the concave surfaces, or flutes, represent a similar evolution of the creases between the bark. When the tree trunks were placed in the temple and the weight of the building was placed on them, sometimes they would split, and to prevent this, a copper collar was shrunk around them at the top. This collar, in the development of time, became the decorative ring around the top of the Doric column. Thus may be seen how a crude thing, used through successive generations, always for the same purpose, has been touched and retouched through the ages by the hand of man, guided by one unseen, until it has come down to us as a thing of beauty.

Taste varies in the beauty of architecture as well as in art generally. Some admire the Gothic cathedrals of Europe, others admire the Taj Mahal in India, and still others prefer the temples of Japan; but to those who admire the architecture of the Greeks and the Romans, the Parthenon is the most beautiful building in the world. Regardless, however, of what may be thought of the beauty of its architecture, it is the most perfect. This was brought about through the subtleties and refinements that the Greeks used in the most aesthetic age of the history of the world, by removing optical illusions more completely from the Parthenon than from any other building. That is the secret of its supremacy in an architectural sense, as well as the source of much of its beauty. These subtleties and refinements were the result of the experience of the ages, plus the age in which the Parthenon was built, plus the master hand of Phidias who built it.

The age of Pericles has been known through the centuries as the "Golden Age of Greece," but the judgment of time has forced us to the conclusion that it was also the golden age of the world in so far as the beauty of architecture and sculptural art is concerned. As for Phidias, certainly no one can deny his genius as an executive or his supremacy in the world of art.

There is no more intriguing part of the whole narrative of the Parthenon than this story of the subtlety of the Greeks in overcoming optical illusions and neutralizing differences in distance. The whole story can never be told, as it has not been, and perhaps never will be, fully understood, leaving the Parthenon in beautiful isolation, the acme of architecture for all time.

Perhaps the most important, certainly the most prominent, of the refinements of the Parthenon is the curvature of the horizontal lines. For example, the floor of the Naos is four and a quarter inches higher near the center of the room than it is around the edges, a convex lens of low degree. The Greeks knew that a straight line in juxta-

The Naos or East Room Showing Symmetry of Columns, the Depressed Floor and Some of the Elgin Marbles

position to a curve was inharmonious and to be beautiful a curve must be against a curve. If the floor had been made level in the first place, as it appears, there would have been the straight line of the floor against the curves of the columns on three sides, and the result would have been an optical illusion which would have left it apparently concave. To correct this, the floor was made convex. This neutralized the force of the illusion and left the floor apparently level when, as a matter of fact, it is curved upward. It should be noted that some of the curves of the Parthenon are not parts of a circle, but of a parabola; in this case, the high point of the floor is not exactly in the center. What is true of the floor is true of every horizontal line in the building, inside and out.

The curvature of the horizontal lines is

73

best seen, however, on the outside of the Parthenon, where it is very apparent in the long lines of the corridors, and in the steps of the stylobate. If, however, these are viewed from a distance of fifty or one hundred yards at right angles, they all appear perfectly straight.

It is not true, as some textbooks have it, that there is no straight line in the Parthenon, as there are a number of them; but all of these straight lines are vertical. What should be said is that there are no straight horizontal lines in the Parthenon.

Another refinement used by the Greeks in adding to the beauty of the Parthenon relates to the columns. The visitor to the building is certain to be impressed by the softness of the Doric columns. This is especially true of those of the Naos where their proximity to each other emphasizes their beauty as they are caught banked against each other. When thus seen all other columns fail by comparison and seem as stiff as pokers. This quality of softness is given them by the fact that all the columns, both in the Naos and on the exterior of the building, are different in diameter from those beside them and also spaced differently. These differences are very small, in most instances not more than the sixty-fourth of an inch, and so arranged that each column is different from the one beside it; not sufficiently different to be seen, but rather felt.

The Greeks knew of what is called the vagary of sight. In looking at a column there are two important facts connected with the operation of sight: first the column as it really exists, and second as it is recorded on the retina of the eye. This latter difference varies with each person, infinitesimal to be sure, but different nevertheless. To accommodate the eye to this vagary of sight all the columns of the Parthenon are different, robbing them of their stiffness and adding to their beauty.

Still another refinement which pertains also to the columns is technically known as entasis, which is that quality which gives to them their beautiful symmetry.

In discussing the columns in relation to their softness, it was suggested that they be seen banked against each other. In the discovery of their symmetrical beauty, however, they should be seen singly. When thus seen, the visitor will note that the column apparently rises from the floor at its largest diameter, gradually diminishing in a beautifully fluted shaft, having the very breath of symmetry in every line to the top. That is the way it appears; but, as a matter of fact, it is altogether different. If the column had been constructed as it actually looks, then, instead of being beautifully symmetrical, from an optical illusion, it would have appeared concave at a point just below the center of the column. Knowing this from experience, the Greeks filled in just enough, and no more, to correct the results of the optical illusion and the column is really bulged near the center. It has a smaller diameter at the base, gradually swelling toward the center and then decreasing to the top, yet giving as a result the beautifully symmetrical columns.

It has been noted that the first sight of the Parthenon usually inspires the visitor with a sense of its strength and stability. This effect is produced by another of the subtleties of the Greeks in approaching perfection in the Parthenon. No one without technical knowledge would ever suspect that its columns and walls are other than perpendicular; yet, as a matter of fact, all of them, inside and out, with the exception of the transverse wall dividing the cella into its two rooms, are inclined toward the center. If all were projected on their axes, they would meet in a cluster five thousand eight hundred and fifty-six feet above the base of the temple.

These are by no means all the subtleties and refinements used by the Greeks in eliminating optical illusions and perfecting the beauty of the Parthenon, but those recorded will serve to give the reader a conception of why, throughout the centuries, the Parthenon has commanded the admiration and held the interest of those who have seen it.

One of the major problems that confronted the builders of the Parthenon at Nashville related to the arrangement of the columns of the Naos. Prior to the research work done on the Nashville reproduction, the preponderance of authority favored the theory that the Doric columns of the Naos were monoliths. This matter was settled definitely by the work done by Mr. William Bell Dinsmoor, of New York, who represented the builders in the archaelogical end of the work.

As has been said, nothing remained of the interior of the original Parthenon, after the explosion of 1687 that destroyed it, except the floor and fragments of the walls. One of these fragments happened to be in the end of the building, in the southeast corner of the Naos. Sticking in it, Mr. Dinsmoor discovered a small piece of the architrave and a discoloration of the wall revealing where the rest of it had been. This discovery fixed the fact of an architrave and, following very closely, the further fact that there were two columns superimposed on each other with an architrave between.

After the discovery had been incorporated in the building at Nashville it was perfectly clear that this interpretation was correct. The markings on the floor of the ruin at Athens not only showed where the columns were located, but also disclosed their diameter and order of architecture. The visitor to the Parthenon at Nashville, viewing the columns of the Naos, by the use of his imagination, can easily check the value of Mr. Dinsmoor's discovery; for if the architrave were absent, a monolith no larger in diameter at the base than those seen, and as tall, would have resulted in a shaft so slim as to violate all the harmony of the proportions of the other parts of the building.

The architecture of the Parthenon will always carry with it elements of the mystical and the mysterious to modern minds, accustomed as they are to the solution of engineering problems by rule. Why are the major lines of the Parthenon, apparently parallel, not exactly so? Why not the same length when differing by such slight fractions? These and other questions present themselves for answers that never come. The more the Parthenon is considered, the more interesting it seems.

CHAPTER VI

The Sculptures of the Parthenon

∽✹∾

THE SCULPTURES OF THE PARTHENON
occur in four groups, the Ionic or inner
frieze, the Doric or outer frieze, the east
pediment, and the west pediment. As the
Parthenon itself represents the greatest
achievement of Greek architecture, so the
sculptures of the temple represent the highest expression of Greek art.

In all ages of man the work of the artist
has been recognized as an expression of his
spiritual nature and he has been accorded
a place with the teacher and the preacher,
as one of the links binding the heart of
man to his God. As the subtlety of the
builders of the Parthenon emphasized their

intellect, so the sculptures emphasized their religion. It has already been said that the mythology of the Parthenon is almost the mythology of Greece, consequently the beautiful temple on the Acropolis was a constant reminder to the Athenians of the virtues of their gods.

Let it be noted here that the so-called popular mythology which attributes meanness and licentiousness to the gods is nothing short of slander. In the eyes of the Greeks, the attributes of the gods were those of noble men and women, without their weaknesses and evil tendencies. Even Plato, in his day, is said to have been almost ready to throw Homer away because of his condonement and repetition, to some extent, of this heresy. A characteristic of the Greeks of this period was that, in their art, they always represented their goddesses fully clothed and, almost always, their gods in the nude. This was but an evidence of their respect for women and their fondness for their athletes. Later, the world, with the Greeks, changed its attitude toward this matter.

The Greeks were not idolaters in the sense that they bowed down to gold and ivory. They loved to chisel in marble the beautiful forms that represented to them their gods who dwelt on Mount Olympus. In this, they were not greatly unlike the Christians of the present day who, in some of their churches, delight to have like figures of Jesus and of Mary. Mythical Mount Olympus was just as real to the devout Greek of Pericles' time as an unseen Heaven is to the devout Christian of today.

While the origin of the Parthenon has the most of its roots firmly fixed in Egypt, many of the sculptures were derived from the Assyrians. Particularly is this true of the smaller figures, winged mythical creatures, as well as lions and horses, typical of the Assyrian bas-reliefs. The heavier figures, notably those of the pediments, are essentially Greek.

The ancient Greeks were not given very much to the use of smaller figures on their temples, especially those of the larger type, but liked to fill in the vacant spaces with large figures that could be seen for some distance. This characteristic is exemplified in the sculptures of the Parthenon where some of the larger figures of the pediments weigh as much as a ton.

While Phidias was selected by Pericles for his genius and executive ability as the master mind in the building of the Parthenon, it is but logical to think that his personal connection with the art of the temple was largely confined to its sculptures. It is known that he created the Chryselephantine Statue of Athena, which was a gigantic task in itself. It is thought that in addition to this he may have been the artist of the three Fates of the east pediment. Beyond this, however, it is not reasonable to suppose that he took other than a supervisory part in the work. The Ionic frieze, as a whole, shows evidence of the exclusive planning of one man, and it is easy to conjecture that the man was Phidias. It is out of the question, however, on the grounds of impossibility, to ascribe any of the actual work to him.

In the life and times of Phidias, a love for the beautiful was so general that it was comparable to the air which they breathed. It was not difficult, therefore, for him to find men, some of them almost as accomplished as himself, upon whose shoulders he could lay the greater part of the work. If proof of the aesthetic quality of the age of Pericles is needed, surely it is here. Too often the deeds of those who have led in worthwhile accomplishments emblazon the pages of history, to the exclusion of the heroes who followed. No history of the Parthenon of Pericles should be considered complete without emphasis being placed on the work of all who shared in the glory of its creation.

It is a matter of keen regret that so few of the sculptures of the Parthenon have been preserved; for that reason, in the task of the reproduction of the Parthenon at Nashville, the most difficult problem that presented itself was the reproduction of the sculptures. Particularly is this true of the pedimental sculptures, and the people of the world, as

Interior Corridor, South Side, Showing Elgin Marbles

well as those of America, should be grateful to the artists for the great piece of sculptural work done on the pediments of the Parthenon at Nashville.

When the Parthenon was destroyed in 1687, the sculptures were blown off the temple and, to a great extent, broken up by the explosion. As already noted, only two of the pedimental groups remain on the ruin, one on each pediment; plaster casts of these are now in the British Museum. A much larger proportion of the figures of the friezes remain on the ruin, but they are so badly damaged that identification is practically impossible; this is especially true of the Doric frieze.

In 1801, after the fragments of the sculptures had lain in the debris around the temple for approximately one hundred and fifteen years, Lord Elgin, Minister to Turkey from England, persuaded the Turks, who had again conquered the Greeks, to let him go to Athens and dig up all the sculptures that he could find from around the ruins. He did not, however, limit the work to the recovery of the sculptures alone, but took ten shiploads in all, including two entire columns that had been blown from the peristyle, together with other fragmentary parts of the temple. These he sold to the British government, and they are now the most highly prized possessions of the British Museum, known as the Elgin Marbles.

It was not without difficulty that Lord Elgin disposed of the fragments. Many hasty critics of that day expressed doubt as to their value, and as a result Parliament appointed a committee to investigate the matter before making the purchase. The committee called upon a number of the leading artists of Great Britain to examine the sculptures and make a report. This report was most satisfactory, and thus was preserved to posterity all that remained of what many people regard as the most beautiful sculptural art of all time.

It is popular in some quarters to criticize Lord Elgin for his action in taking the fragments from the Parthenon to England. Some have gone so far as to say that he actually robbed the temple of its sculptures. Unquestionably, the correct view of the matter is that Lord Elgin did the world a great service in salvaging the fragments from the earth in which they had deteriorated for many years and, but for him, might have suffered greater injury. Certain it is, he did not personally profit by the transaction, because firsthand information is that his estate has subsequently been of

91

little value, as he received far less for the sculptures than they cost him.

In the west room of the Parthenon at Nashville, and along the corridors of the east room, may be seen casts which form the only complete set of the pedimental sculptures outside of the British Museum. Many isolated groups of these may be found in America and in Europe, but only at Nashville may all of them be seen. Here they are mounted on wooden bases and form a most interesting exhibit.

In the east room of the Parthenon, at the west end of the south corridor, may be seen the head of one of Selene's steeds, which is considered by many as the finest example of a horse's head in the world. Just beyond, through the door at the end of the corridor, is seen, in the west room, the figure of Heracles. It is interesting to note that in the report of the artists who passed on the value of the Elgin marbles, a statement was incorporated to the effect that the back muscles of the Heracles represented the finest example of physiological art known to the world of that day. Again, another most interesting group of sculptures is seen nearby, in the west end of the east room, the three Fates. This group, which, as we have seen, is thought to be the work of Phidias, is generally regarded as one of the most beautiful examples of sculptural art existing today.

The casts of the Elgin marbles in the Parthenon at Nashville were made by the British government and were not primarily obtained as an exhibit, but as a study for the reproduction of those sculptures now on the building. However, it was not thought inappropriate to mount the fragments and use them as an exhibit, so as to permit visitors to compare the completed figures with them. The comparison can only cover approximately half the figures on the pediments, as the remainder have been lost beyond recovery. Quite naturally, the question is set up in the mind of the reader as to how it was possible for the artists to reproduce all of them.

In 1674, just thirteen years before the explosion which destroyed the Parthenon, young Jacques Carrey, a French artist attached to the French embassy to Turkey, on a voyage from Paris to Constantinople with the ambassador, stopped off at Athens and sketched the temple sculptures. How fortunate! It seems as though the gods themselves were fighting to prevent the loss of the most beautiful work they had ever inspired the Greeks to create. These sketches are preserved in the National Library at Paris and were made available for the artists. From a study of the Elgin marbles, the Carrey drawings, supplemented by further study of Greek contemporary art and of Greek history, which played a large part in it, the artists at Nashville have succeeded in making a wonderful reproduction of the Parthenon's sculptures.

In speaking of the sculptures of the Parthenon at Nashville, particularly those of the pediments, it is conceded that the word "reproduction" does not tell the whole story, but the tendency on the part of some commentators to refer to them as "re-creations" is correct only in part. The study before indicated permitted the artists, within a wide circle of probability, to reproduce the greater part of the figures as they were originally. However, not all of them were even subject to possibility. When Jacques Carrey came to sketch the figures of the east pediment, he found a yawning gap for a distance of forty feet in the center of the pediment where the figures should have been. What became of this section of the sculptures is purely in the realm of speculation; one guess seems as good as another. Various theories have been advanced to account for their loss, the best of which, perhaps, is the thought that when the Turks came to build minarets on the temple, one of them was erected directly through the center of the pediment and the broken sculptures were burned for lime. At any rate, they have never been seen since the Turkish conquest, and it is highly improbable that they ever will.

The re-creation of the lost sculptures of the east pediment presented to the artists the greatest problem of their work on the Parthenon, and its solution represented much intense study and most careful work. It is interesting to note the data upon which they relied for the re-creation, as follows: Pausanius, a Greek historian and traveler, writing in the second century after Christ, before the hand of man or of time had changed the building in any way, made the significant statement, "What is seen on the pediment on entering the temple relates to the birth of Athena; at the back is the contest of Poseidon and Athena for the land." This statement furnished the artists with the basic themes of the pediments. Since the entire east pediment is ninety-four feet in length, there were fifty-four feet intact up to the time of the explosion that wrecked the building. The Elgin marbles and the Carrey drawings reveal those remaining

97

figures as all pointing to the same thing, the birth of Athena and her reign. With this information, and making use of the knowledge gained from the west pediment as an aid in determining the position of the figures on the pediment, the artists at Nashville, Belle Kinney and her husband, Leopold Scholz, who collaborated in the work, reached up into the blue sky and pulled down the magnificent creation of the lost section of the east pediment sculptures. It is certain that if Phidias should return to the earth, and view this re-creation of his cherished work, he would not be ashamed of what he would see.

To the student of Greek mythology, Greek history, and Greek art, the sculptures of the Parthenon at Nashville present a most interesting study.

CHAPTER VII

The Ionic and Doric Friezes

⟨∿⟩

THE INNER OR IONIC FRIEZE, sometimes erroneously called *the* frieze, was one of the most beautiful of the groups of sculptures on the original Parthenon. It was almost unknown to distinctly Doric temples and owes its place on the Parthenon to some one or more Ionic temples from which the idea was without doubt copied.

In the Ionic frieze is found most of the atmosphere of ancient Assyria that is associated with the Parthenon. This frieze was low in relief, forty inches in height, and of necessity the figures of the men and women and animals which went to make it up were small, typical of the Assyrian bas-reliefs.

The Ionic frieze was located along the outer walls of the Parthenon, extending forty inches down from the top of the wall, and rested on a blue fret running all around the building, a distance of five hundred and twenty-four feet. It was a marvelous piece of sculptural art; and although there were approximately as many as six hundred figures in the frieze—men, women, and animals—no two of them were alike, no two men, no two women, and no two animals; yet all were graceful, dignified, and beautiful.

Located as it was high up on the outer walls of the building, and inside the great Doric columns of the peristyle, the architrave at the top of the columns, and the columns themselves, cut off almost all the light from above, so that the frieze was dependent on that from below. Those conditions afforded the Greeks an opportunity to display, in their sculptural work, some of the subtlety that is so apparent in the architecture of the Parthenon. Of necessity the light, striking the lower part of the frieze first, would have accentuated it and made it altogether out of proportion to the rest, and the effect would have been poor. To neutralize this, the Greeks gave a sharper cutting to the top part of the figures, to which the light reached last, and also set that part of the frieze a little further out from the background, thus promoting a harmonious whole.

The entire Ionic frieze discloses the master hand of one man as to its general design, but at the same time it negatived the idea that any one, or even a dozen men, could have executed the work as a whole.

The Ionic frieze of the Parthenon de-

picted the Panathenaic Procession which oc-
curred every four years in Athens. It was
an established part of the Panathenaic Fes-
tival and coincident also with the athletic
contests held in honor of Athena. On this
occasion the Greeks assembled themselves in
the downtown streets of Athens; men and
women of high and low degree with their
slaves, various kinds of animals, chariots
with their horsemen, men at arms, wild
horses led by Barbarians, dignitaries of state
and maidens. These formed a procession
which wound its way up through the streets
of Athens leading to the Acropolis, on to
that sacred hill, and into the Parthenon
where they invested the figure of Athena
with a peplos, or robe, which had been
woven by the women of Athens during the
previous four-year period. It was at once
a gala and a solemn occasion for the Greeks.

102

The Ionic frieze, whose figures portrayed this procession in stone, was so marvelously wrought that it gave the impression of motion. It was arranged in a series of overlapping sections in such a manner as to cause the onlooker, as he gazed upward, to almost see the men and women and animals marching along.

Unfortunately and regrettably, for lack of funds, the Ionic frieze has been left off the Parthenon at Nashville, which lacks that much of being completed. It is available, however, as the greater part of it is in the British Museum, some in the Louvre, and the remainder, twenty-four feet in all, is still on the ruin at Athens. It is all in good condition except that on the old building which is almost past recognition and will be difficult to reproduce accurately. There is no doubt that the Ionic frieze will eventually find its place on the temple at Nashville.

The Doric, or outer frieze, is seen on the Parthenon on the outside of the building above the architrave that rests on the great Doric columns of the peristyle. It extends along both sides of the building and underneath the pedimental sculptures at each end. It consists of a repeating conventional design, called a triglyph, which divides the frieze into ninety-two panels, each panel containing a group of sculptures. The panels with their sculptures are known as the metopes and are approximately four feet square.

In the building of the older Greek temples there was always an open space between the architrave and the top of the beams upon which the roof was supported and which also prevented the walls from spread-

ing. There is at least one record of a person confined as a prisoner in one of the ancient Doric temples, making his escape through one of these openings. Later, the Doric frieze served the purpose of camouflaging this unsightly space, transforming it into a beautiful feature of the temple. The ends of the crossbeams were covered by the triglyphs (thrice cloven), contributing to this result. The sculptures of the Doric frieze with their sharp curves served admirably as a foil for the straight lines of the triglyphs and the square appearance of the metopes; they are in high relief.

There were no repetitions in the sculptures of the Doric frieze. They told legendary and mythological stories that were dear to the heart of the Greeks. That part of the frieze on the eastern end of the building pictured scenes from the struggle between the gods and the giants. The war between the Greeks and the Amazons was shown by the figures of the frieze on the western end. On the north side of the building the figures depicted incidents of the Trojan War, while those along the south side told the story of the Lapiths, a tribe of the Greeks, and the Centaurs. The story is that of a Princess of this tribe who was to be married. She sent invitations to the Centaurs, mythological creatures, part man and part horse, to come to the wedding feast. They came, drank wine, became drunken, and insulted the bride, which brought on a war in which the Centaurs were defeated.

Of the sculptures of the Doric frieze, only those of the south side of the original Parthenon have been sufficiently preserved to admit of their reproduction with any degree of accuracy. It was for this reason that the builders of the Parthenon at Nashville thought best not to attempt to reproduce them all, but to treat the entire frieze as an extension of that of the south side. This course, of necessity, called for a repetition of the figures on the other three sides; but the treatment at Nashville has been so skillfully done as not to mar the harmony of the whole, and in the judgment of the critics has produced an effect far superior to any that might have been attained by an attempt at the impossible.

The figures of the Doric frieze are archaic and stiff by comparison with those of the pedimental sculptures, or of the Ionic frieze, and are thought, therefore, not to be the work of Phidias and his associates, but rather a transfer from one of the earlier temples to the Parthenon. They play their part well in the harmonious whole and reflect the ability and genius of Phidias, who adapted them.

The Naos or East Room as Seen Through the Eastern Doors

CHAPTER VIII

The West Pediment

⟡

As has been indicated, the reproduction and re-creation of the sculptures of the pediments of the Parthenon was most difficult. It represented years of intense study and research, much travel and investigation. Above all, it represented a tireless spirit and an unflagging love for the work on the part of the artists, inspiring them to produce the magnificent results shown on the pediments at Nashville.

The figures of the west pediment were more easily reproduced than those of the east pediment, as they were more completely authenticated by the Elgin marbles and the Carrey drawings. The markings on the base of the west pediment were also more revealing as to the position of the figures, for the reason that it was not injured prior to the destruction of the Parthenon in 1687 as was the less fortunate east pediment.

It should be understood that the explosion that destroyed the Parthenon did its greatest damage to the figures themselves rather than to the base on which they rested, and as a consequence less difficulty was encountered by the artists in placing the sculptures in their proper settings on the west than on the east pediment. In considering the sculptures of the two pediments, it must also be borne in mind that the force of the explosion was greatest in the eastern portion of the building, as evidenced by the condition of the ruin, and for that reason also the greatest damage was to the east pediment.

The sculptures of the west pediment tell

the story of the struggle between Poseidon, the powerful god of the sea, and his niece Athena, the goddess of wisdom, for the possession of Attica, or ancient Greece.

In the center of the pediment, to the right, is seen the heroic figure of Poseidon with his three-pronged weapon, or trident, in his hand, and his friends and supporters to his right. Opposing him, and to the left, is the equally heroic figure of Athena with her great spear in her hand and her supporters to her left. Both these gods coveted the fair land of Attica and wanted the worship of its people. They were unable to agree and appealed to the gods for a decision. The gods held their convocation on the Acropolis, the site of the Parthenon, and this assembly is shown by the figures of the west pediment.

Next to Poseidon, to his right, is seen his

wife, Amphitrite, who was also his charioteer, driving his chariot. Amphitrite was
the most celebrated of the fifty daughters
of Nereus, a genial old man of the sea.
These beautiful daughters of Nereus were
known as the Nereids and played a large
part in Grecian mythology. In front of
Amphitrite is the figure of a beautiful
winged Nereid. While no chariot is shown,
the presence of the horses, together with
Amphitrite's pose and dress, renders it easy
for the imagination to fill it in around her.
The province of the winged figure, as is
also indicated by its pose, is to lend en-
couragement to Poseidon and perhaps act as
a messenger.

The next group on the pediment is that
of the princess Tyro and her two sons whose
father was Poseidon. Pelias is on her left
and Neleus on her right.

The West Pediment Showing Section of Doric Frieze Underneath the Acroteria Above

The next figure to the right is the unfortunate Ino with her son, Melicertes, on her knee. Next to her is seen Thalassa, a personification of the sea and therefore appropriately found among the friends of Poseidon.

On Thalassa's right is seen Cephissus, the god of the Cephissus river near Athens, and last, at the extreme south end of the pediment, is shown the water nymph Callirrhoë who guarded constantly Athena's spring; she was the only adherent of Athena among the groups of the south end of the pediment.

Near the center of the pediment, on the left of Athena, are shown her chariot and steeds. Both Athena's horses and those of Poseidon, as seen on the pediment, are among the finest examples of sculpture created by present-day artists. They are partial recreations, as they are not represented in the

Elgin marbles but are found among the Carrey drawings. In the chariot is Erechtheus, Athena's foster son and charioteer. Erechtheus was the second mythical king of Athens. Beside the chariot is seen Hermes, who appears to be encouraging Athena's friends and perhaps holding himself in readiness to act as her messenger.

Directly behind Athena's chariot, toward the north end of the pediment, is seen a group consisting of Cecrops (farthest from the chariot) and his daughters Pandrosos, Herse, and Aglauros, with the diminutive Eros between the two latter.

The aged and feeble Cecrops is being supported by a staff in his right hand and his daughter Pandrosos on his left. Cecrops was the founder and first mythical king of Athens. He is said to have presided over the contest between Poseidon and Athena.

As has been noted elsewhere, fragments of the figures of Cecrops and Pandrosos are the only sculptures now remaining on the west pediment at Athens. The sculptural work on these two figures, as shown by the fragments, is inferior to that of the rest of the pediment and the figures are therefore thought to be a transfer from an earlier temple. Plaster casts of them are in the British Museum and in the Parthenon at Nashville.

Pandrosos, Herse, and Aglauros were personifications of Dew and its healthful influences. In this group Eros appears to be greatly interested in what is taking place and is receiving the attention of Herse and Aglauros. He is the god of love, the son of Athena, and, naturally, was one of her partisans.

To the left of Cecrops, in the extreme

north angle of the pediment, is seen the
figure of the river god Ilissus. The plaster
cast in the Parthenon at Nashville, and the
reproduction on the pediment, disclose this
to be second only to the Heracles as a speci-
men of sculptural perfection of the human
form.

It is difficult to understand the signifi-
cance of the two river gods, Ilissus and
Cephissus, the one on the extreme north end
and the other on the extreme south end of
the pediment. It is thought, however, that
the two rivers which were adjacent to
Athens, probably marked the boundaries of
the land contested for by Poseidon and
Athena.

As a result of the convocation, the gods
decreed that the contestant who should bless
Greece the most would be given the control
of Athens and have the worship of the

Greeks. It was to be a battle of blessing, rather than of blood.

Poseidon, in granting his blessing, struck the solid rock of the Acropolis with his trident; and as he was the god of the sea, it obeyed him and came up in a rushing, gushing spring of salt water, symbolic of the promise he made them that if they would make him their god he would make of them a mighty maritime nation; their glory should be on the sea. When it became Athena's turn to grant her blessing, she stuck her great spear in the earth and withdrew it, and from the place sprang an olive tree, the parent of all those which have so greatly blessed Greece from that day to this. The gods acting wisely, as they always did, decreed that Athena's gift was of far greater advantage to the Athenians and the Greeks than any promise of the glory of war, as

117

made by Poseidon, and made her the patron goddess of Athens.

Certainly the lesson of compromise, of peace, and of thrift, as taught by the beautiful west pediment, is opportunely retold to a storm-tossed world by the Parthenon at Nashville.

CHAPTER IX

The East Pediment

IT WOULD BE VERY DIFFICULT for a visitor to Nashville to decide which group of sculptures on the Parthenon is the most lovely. Each general group fits so harmoniously into its own particular place, that a choice of one could not avoid being unfair to the others. Viewing the west pediment first, the person essaying judgment might exclaim, "What could be more beautiful!" Yet on leaving it and looking at the east pediment he might easily be found saying, "Here is the answer." The presence on the east pediment of the three Fates, the Heracles, and the steeds of Selene, probably gives it the advantage over the other groups,

119

especially in the eyes of the artists. The rhythm wrought by Phidias into the position of the figures on the pediments at Athens is easily discernible at Nashville.

Occasionally a well-informed visitor to the Parthenon at Nashville will ask if the re-creation of the lost section of the east pediment is not a matter of guesswork. The answer is, that intelligent conjecture fits the case better, and, in the light of the beautiful work itself, is usually satisfying.

The story of the east pediment is very beautiful and tells of the birth of Athena and her reign. In the beginning, Zeus, the father of the gods, the king of the gods, had a very severe headache and could find no relief. He had long wanted a child born of the intellect. He had thrown out of Heaven his son Hephaestus, because he had been born with a maimed foot. It is said

The East Pediment with Section of the Doric Frieze Underneath Showing Gryphon Monsters and Acroteria on Roof

that he was so disappointed at having a son born maimed, that he threw him out of Heaven, and it took a whole day for him to fall from the heavens to the earth. Hephaestus was the god of fire, the god of metals, the blacksmith of the gods. He forged the thunderbolts that Zeus used in his battles of Heaven. He sent word to his father that if he would restore him to his rightful position among the gods, he would cure him of his headache. Thereupon, Zeus assembled the gods on Mount Olympus. As has been said before, the assembly of the gods of the west pediment was on the Acropolis, but here—in the home of the gods. From somewhere, in a thundercloud, came Hephaestus and struck his father in the back of his head with an axe; from the wound, giving him his wish, sprang Athena, fully grown and clothed and armed. She was announced and crowned goddess of wisdom by Nike, goddess of victory, who winged her way in from the great somewhere. It is said that at this event the earth groaned, Mount Olympus trembled, and the gods stood in amazement at the miracle that had been performed. These four figures form the highest pinnacle of the east pediment of the Parthenon.

At the extreme south end of the pediment, representing the beginning of the reign of Athena, is seen in the morning Helios, the god of the sun, the god of the morning, coming up out of the sea, driving his four steeds representing the four seasons. As the horses come bounding out of the sea, Helios can scarcely restrain them, so eager are they to mount the skies—the sun god coming out of the sea. As they do so, Heracles, the next figure on the pediment, is shown with his club on his shoulder, nonchalantly looking at the horses, paying no attention to what is taking place on Mount Olympus. He is looking at the sun as it rises. Heracles was known as the favorite of the gods. In his early manhood they had permitted him to choose between virtue on the one hand, and vice on the other, both very attractively arrayed. He chose virtue rather than vice, and thus became their favorite. He did many heroic deeds in Grecian history, and was the national hero of Greece. Heracles was himself made a god; Zeus was his father, his mother was a mortal.

Next, on the pediment, may be seen the figures of Demeter, the sister of Zeus, and her daughter Persephone. Demeter was the goddess of the seasons. Ceres was her Roman name, and her daughter, Persephone, was the goddess of the underworld. She became the goddess of the underworld in this wise: One day when Persephone was in the fields plucking violets with her maidens, suddenly the earth opened and through it, in a chariot, came Pluto, the god of Hades. He saw her, fell in love with her, seized her, took her back to Hades, and made her his queen. Her mother grieved sorely and would not be comforted. She had powerful influence with the gods. She sent plagues on the earth and worried the gods, until Zeus was forced to compel Pluto to bring Persephone back to her mother. Thereafter, it is said, under a compromise agreement, Persephone spent six months of each year with her mother among the gods, and six months with her husband, Pluto, in Hades.

The next figure on the pediment is that of Iris, the female messenger of the gods, the rainbow goddess. She is represented on the pediment as being poised, ready to go at a moment's notice, to tell the story of the birth of Athena to the world. This is the first figure seen among the fragments as the visitor enters the Parthenon door, and is often confused with the Winged Victory of Samothrace. The confusion arises from the fact that in the fragment of the Parthenon figure of Iris, located in the west room, she is holding her scarf at arm's length in her hands and the fragment is broken through the scarf and through the arms, causing it to look as if it might be a wing, when, as a matter of fact, it is the fragment of a scarf and not a wing; and the figure is not the Winged Victory, but is Iris, the female messenger of the gods, the rainbow goddess.

Next is seen on the pediment the figure

125

of Poseidon, the god of the sea; Neptune was his Roman name. Poseidon was the brother of Zeus, one of the chief deities of the Greeks, and is represented on the east pediment as sitting calmly by, looking on at what is taking place.

The next figure beyond Poseidon is that of Aphrodite, or Venus, the goddess of beauty, the goddess of love. She seems shocked at what she sees, and shrinks a little; but is comforting Hebe, the goddess of youth, who is reclining at her feet, by placing her hand on her head.

Then comes the central group, Hephaestus, Zeus, Nike, and Athena, or Minerva as the Romans called her, illustrating the story of the birth of Athena.

On Athena's right is seen Ares, or Mars, the god of war. He is represented on the pediment as looking rather sternly past

Athena as though he does not welcome this additional warlike member to the family of the gods.

The next figure is that of Artemis, the twin sister of Apollo. Artemis is the goddess of the fields, the goddess of hunting; Diana is her Roman name. She is represented on the pediment as shading her eyes with her hand from the resplendent glory of the newborn goddess.

Just beyond Artemis is seen Hera, queen of Heaven, also known as Juno, the jealous wife of Zeus. In addition to her jealousy, it is said that she was vain and the peacock, seen near by, was sacred to her. Hera was also the goddess of maternity, and very fittingly was present at the birth of Athena.

The next figure is that of Hermes, the male messenger of the gods, corresponding to Iris, the female messenger. Iris usually

127

executed the commands and carried the messages for Hera, while Hermes performed a like office for Zeus. He is always represented with a magic wand, or caduceus, in his hand, which was given to him by Apollo. One day, when Hermes was a mere child, almost a baby, he was playing in the fields and captured a tortoise. He placed strings across the shell of the tortoise and made a musical instrument (we call it the lyre), and presented it to his brother Apollo. Apollo, who was the god of music, was so delighted with the precociousness of his baby brother that he gave him the magic wand, which had the power of putting gods and mortals to sleep at his will. Hermes is also shown with wings on his ankles and wings on his cap. He was the god of business, and also the god of transportation. His figure adorns many of the railway sta-

128

Floor of Treasury or West Room Showing Arrangement of Ionic Columns and Figures from Elgin Marbles of Iris and Heracles

tions of the world. His Roman name is Mercury.

Beyond Hermes, on the pediment, is seen Apollo, the god of music, with his harp. He was also the god of manly youth and the god of healing. Esculapius, his son, was the first doctor of Greece, the father of all the physicians. Apollo was regarded as the most beautiful of the gods. Reclining on him is seen Ganymede, the cupbearer of the gods.

These were the chief deities of the Greeks. There were others which they worshiped also. They were as sacred to the ancient Greek as Jehovah is to us, and it is pertinent to say that they worshiped the beautiful— and the beautiful is the spiritual.

We are not so much interested in the gods of the Greeks in this twentieth century, however, as we are in human life;

129

and the next group of figures to the right of Apollo and Ganymede, the three Fates, brings the whole matter closer to us, because it represents the Greek idea of life. The first figure in the group is Clotho, who is represented as spinning the thread of life; and as she spins, the second figure, Lachesis, winds it on a spool, and the third figure, Atropos, clips it at will, typifying the beginning, the span, and the end of life—the destiny of us all.

Last, in the extreme south angle of the pediment, in the evening, is seen the gentle Selene, the goddess of the moon, the goddess of the evening, guiding her tired steeds, so different from those that are seen coming out of the sea in the morning, down into the cool, quiet waters of the deep, typifying not alone the close of the day, but the close of the reign of Athena, and the end of time.

ITS REPRODUCTION IN AMERICA

The gods of the Greeks are no more. They have no single worshiper left in all the face of the earth today to pay them homage, yet their deeds are told in song and story, and their memory is green in the hearts of those who love the beautiful.

CHAPTER X

Conclusion

AND NOW, WE COME to the close of the story of the Parthenon.

The period of Pericles marked one of the high points in the history of the world. A comparison of its characteristics serves to emphasize its superiority over other epochs in many ways. One of the glaring faults in modern effort in art is an overemphasis of originality. Of this the Greeks were innocent. They were not extravagant in anything. Their calm pursuit of excellence was not influenced greatly by every wind that blew. No passing cult became a "craze." It has been said that the Hellene always possessed judgment in imagination, intellect in sentiment, and reflection in passion.

The Parthenon at Athens was not merely a wonderful building, but an expression of Greek mind and heart. It did not spring up in a day as did Athena from the head of Zeus, but, as we have seen, found its roots in the prehistoric altars of their goddess. It was not built to please individuals, but to honor their gods. It is no wonder, then, that when it came into full flower in the "Age of Pericles," it should have reached that state which the judgment of succeeding generations has pronounced perfection.

The Parthenon, which epitomized deep religious feeling and characterized one of the greatest periods in the world's history, has had many lessons for the generations that have come after it. If such is not the case, of what value then is excellence? Our lives are wasted for those who follow. No doubt the Parthenon as it stood out upon the Acropolis inspired the Greeks to higher and better things. Down through the centuries, the Greek boy, as he turned to it in the morning, has made new resolves to achieve a higher life. Even when, later, the Greeks fell upon evil days, amid all the discouragements and results of counterinfluences that beset them as a nation, assuredly the old ruin that still looks down upon Athens has served to keep the spirit of the days of a bygone glory alive in their hearts. No better proof of this is found than in the visits of cultured Greeks from Athens to the Parthenon at Nashville. It is a joy to those who love the finer things of life, to see the glistening eyes and hear the emotion-filled voices as, for the first time in their lives, they behold the Parthenon as it looked

135

to their ancestors. Such experiences lead us to believe that in the great family of nations, which a future civilization is sure to see, Greece will be found among them with her head held high, proud of the part which she has played.

The Parthenon at Nashville stands alone as a portrayal of the Parthenon of Pericles. It would be too much of a challenge to the antiquity of the Parthenon, to say that every statement made about it in these pages bears the stamp of absolute authenticity. It can be said, however, that because of all the facts obtained from the research and records of earlier days, and of the eleven years of research and study in our own times, the Parthenon at Nashville will stand, in the judgment of time, as the last word. Little, if anything possible, remains unknown. In these pages, where there has been any doubt, it has been so stated, and it is hoped that no one will consider the picture overdrawn. In any case, the critic is not in a strong position until he stands before the Parthenon at Athens, and its beautiful reproduction at Nashville.

It is difficult to estimate the influence of the Parthenon at Nashville on the world of today. To those who love the beautiful, either by instinct or cultivation, the Parthenon is a thing to be revered; to others it is just another building. Some who enter the building for the first time are overcome, some are unimpressed. Of those who come to criticize, many remain to praise.

To understand and appreciate the Parthenon, it must be studied. At some buildings we may glance and pass on, but not so with the Parthenon. It is compelling. A revelation of its balanced lines and harmony of proportions, its simplicity, both delicate and strong, its subtleties, some bordering on the mystical, marks the Parthenon as a thing by itself.

The people of America are realizing more and more the value of the beautiful and demanding its recognition. The Parthenon is playing a large part in this, let us say, new birth. It has become the mecca of thousands of people whose enthusiasm causes other thousands to follow, making it known and loved throughout the Western world and inculcating everywhere a love for the beautiful.

There is no question as to the influence of the Parthenon on those who live in its environs. Nashville was a cultured city in 1931; largely through the influence of the Parthenon it will be much more so in 1951.

The Parthenon is used only for educational and cultural purposes. Lectures are delivered to schools, colleges, and cultural organizations from time to time, covering its history, architecture, and sculptures, and twice each week to the general public. Teachers in the schools and colleges of Nashville bring their classes every year for these lectures and others come from more distant points. In the last fiscal year sixty-two college, ninety-five high school, and eighty-eight primary school groups visited the Parthenon.

This, then, may be said of the Parthenon: As in the earlier days, even so now, young and old, rich and poor, are alike made happy by its sheer beauty, and inspired by its history to reach up for a higher and better life.

"In the elder days of Art,
 Builders wrought with greatest care
Each minute and unseen part;
 For the Gods see everywhere.

Let us do our work as well,
 Both the unseen and the seen;
Make the house, where Gods may dwell,
 Beautiful, entire, and clean." [1]

[1] From "The Builders," by H. W. Longfellow.
Used by permission of, and by arrangement with,
Houghton Mifflin Company.